Written Calculation
Addition
Answers

Schofield & Sims

Schofield & Sims | Written Calculation: Addition Answers

Introduction for parents and teachers

This book provides correct answers to all the questions in the Pupil Book **Written Calculation: Addition** (ISBN 978 07217 1266 6), including those contained in each **Check-up test** and **Final test**.

Which pupils will benefit most from Written Calculation: Addition?

Addition is for pupils who already understand the value of digits in numbers. They are able to identify the units digit in a four-digit number such as 5468. They also know the values of the other digits, including tens, hundreds and thousands. Pupils should also be experienced in adding and subtracting single-digit numbers and should know their number bonds to 20 (for example, 7 + 8, 9 + 5, 14 + 6). Pupils who know these well will find written addition easier than those who have to work them out. For this reason, pupils who have not yet memorised number bonds may find it useful temporarily to refer to a list of number facts – downloadable from the Schofield & Sims website. This will allow them to focus on the procedures of the written method. Once the pupils are familiar with the facts, they will no longer need the list.

How should the Pupil Book be used?

Pupils should work consecutively through all 18 'steps', if they are to become fully proficient in the most important stages of the learning process. At the end of each step are **Problem solving** questions. Pupils record their workings onto the grids provided and also write their answers in the book. Make sure that each pupil completes the **self-evaluation** rating at the end of each step by ticking 'Easy', 'OK' or 'Difficult'. Review each pupil's rating against his or her score for that step, and give support to pupils who are struggling. The final steps in the book extend more able pupils and take them beyond the statutory aspects of written addition, requiring them to work with larger numbers and decimals, for example. **Check-up tests** and a **Final test** help you to monitor progress, and this book of **Answers** makes marking simple and quick. Use the **conversion chart** at the end of each test to quickly convert the pupil's score to a percentage that can be recorded and used to measure progress.

Please note: Pupils will require additional squared paper to help them complete some of the pages in the Pupil Book.

The separate **Written Calculation: Teacher's Guide** (ISBN 978 07217 1278 9) contains full teaching notes and assessment resources. The **Teacher's Resource Book** (ISBN 978 07217 1300 7) contains photocopiable resources. Both cover the whole series and provide the teacher with valuable guidance and resources to support the teaching of written calculation. For free downloads and for further details on all the other **Written Calculation** books, visit **www.schofieldandsims.co.uk**

Published by Schofield & Sims Ltd, Dogley Mill, Fenay Bridge, Huddersfield HD8 0NQ, UK Tel 01484 607080 www.schofieldandsims.co.uk
First published in 2015. Copyright © Schofield & Sims Ltd, 2015.
Authors: **Hilary Koll and Steve Mills**
Hilary Koll and Steve Mills have asserted their moral rights under the Copyright, Designs and Patents Act, 1988, to be identified as the authors of this work.
British Library Cataloguing in Publication Data
A catalogue record for this book is available from the British Library.
All rights reserved. No part of this publication may be reproduced, stored in a retrieval system, or transmitted in any form or by any means, electronic, mechanical, photocopying, recording or otherwise, without either the prior permission of the publisher or a licence permitting restricted copying in the United Kingdom issued by the Copyright Licensing Agency Limited, Saffron House, 6–10 Kirby Street, London EC1N 8TS.
Commissioned by **Carolyn Richardson Publishing Services (www.publiserve.co.uk)**
Design by **Ledgard Jepson Ltd**
Cover illustration by **Joe Hance (joehance.co.uk)**
Printed in the UK by **Wyndeham Gait Ltd, Grimsby, Lincolnshire**
ISBN 978 07217 1272 7

Contents

Step 1	**Two-digit addition** no carrying	4
Step 2	**Three-digit addition** no carrying	6
Step 3	**Three-digit addition** carrying 1 ten	8
Step 4	**Three-digit addition** carrying 1 hundred	10
Step 5	**Three-digit addition** carrying once, including answers greater than 999	12
Step 6	**Three-digit addition of three numbers** carrying once	14
Check-up test 1	**Two- and three-digit addition, including carrying once**	16
Step 7	**Four-digit addition** carrying once	18
Step 8	**Three-digit addition** carrying twice	20
Step 9	**Four-digit addition** carrying once or twice	22
Step 10	**Three- and four-digit addition** carrying once or twice, answers greater than 9999	24
Step 11	**Four-digit addition** carrying three times	26
Step 12	**Addition of three numbers with three and four digits** carrying up to three times	28
Check-up test 2	**Three- and four-digit addition, with up to three carries**	30
Step 13	**Five-digit addition** carrying up to four times	32
Step 14	**Addition of a list of numbers**	34
Step 15	**Large number addition**	36
Check-up test 3	**Addition of large numbers**	38
Step 16	**Decimal addition** one decimal place	40
Step 17	**Decimal addition** two decimal places	42
Step 18	**Decimal addition** different numbers of decimal places	44
Final test	**Addition of whole numbers and decimals**	46

Step 1: Two-digit addition no carrying

When learning written addition, it is important to know how to set numbers out vertically with the correct digits in the correct columns. Here, 56 and 33 are correctly written under the Tens and Units headings.

What to do

1. Set out the numbers in the correct columns with one digit in each square.

2. Always start at the right-hand side, with the units column! Add the top and bottom digits. 6 + 3 = 9

3. Next move to the left and look at the digits in the tens column. Add the top and bottom digits. 5 tens + 3 tens = 8 tens

4. Finally, look at the answer and check whether it seems a sensible answer. You can subtract one of the numbers in the question from the answer to see if it gives you the other number. 89 − 33 = 56. Yes, this is correct.

56 + 33 = ?

	T	U
	5	6
+	3	3

	T	U
	5	6
+	3	3
		9

	T	U
	5	6
+	3	3
	8	9

	T	U
	8	9
−	3	3
	5	6

Now you try

1 25 + 44 = ?

	T	U
	2	5
+	4	4
	6	9

2 47 + 31 = ?

	T	U
	4	7
+	3	1
	7	8

3 61 + 25 = ?

	T	U
	6	1
+	2	5
	8	6

4 54 + 23 = ?

	T	U
	5	4
+	2	3
	7	7

5 77 + 22 = ?

	T	U
	7	7
+	2	2
	9	9

6 53 + 45 = ?

	T	U
	5	3
+	4	5
	9	8

Schofield & Sims | Written Calculation: Addition Answers 5

More practice
Set out these questions yourself to answer them.

7 35 + 54 = ?

```
  T U
  3 5
+ 5 4
─────
  8 9
```

8 65 + 23 = ?

```
  T U
  6 5
+ 2 3
─────
  8 8
```

9 38 + 41 = ?

```
  T U
  3 8
+ 4 1
─────
  7 9
```

Problem solving

10 Ahmed bought a T-shirt costing £23 and a pair of jeans costing £42. What was the total cost?

```
    2 3
+   4 2
───────
    6 5
```
£65

11 Find the total of 24 and 72.

```
    2 4
+   7 2
───────
    9 6
```
96

12 Dina is 23 years old. Her gran is 46 years older than she is. How old is her gran?

```
    2 3
+   4 6
───────
    6 9
```
69

13 The height of Li's cat is 23cm. Li's dog is 61cm taller than her cat. What is the height of Li's dog?

```
    2 3
+   6 1
───────
    8 4
```
84cm

14 Sam collects stickers. He has 45 stickers in one book and 52 in another. How many stickers is that altogether?

```
    4 5
+   5 2
───────
    9 7
```
97

15 What is the sum of 36 and 62?

```
    3 6
+   6 2
───────
    9 8
```
98

How did I find Step 1?   ☐ Easy   ☐ OK   ☐ Difficult

Step 2: Three-digit addition no carrying

For three-digit numbers, work in the same way. Make sure the numbers are set out in the correct columns in the same way. Here, 526 and 143 are correctly written under the Hundreds, Tens and Units headings.

What to do

526 + 143 = ?

1. Set out the numbers in the correct columns with one digit in each square.

2. Always start at the right-hand side, with the units column! Add both units digits. 6 + 3 = 9

3. Next move to the left and look at the digits in the tens column. Add both tens digits. 2 + 4 = 6

4. Then move to the left again and add both hundreds digits. 5 + 1 = 6

5. Finally, look at the answer and check whether it seems a sensible answer. 669 − 143 = 526, which is correct!

Now you try

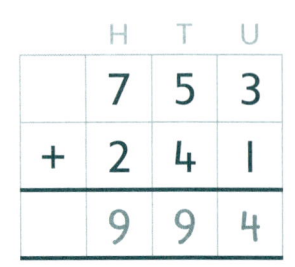

1 483 + 414 = ?

	H	T	U
	4	8	3
+	4	1	4
	8	9	7

2 575 + 214 = ?

	H	T	U
	5	7	5
+	2	1	4
	7	8	9

3 652 + 325 = ?

	H	T	U
	6	5	2
+	3	2	5
	9	7	7

4 753 + 241 = ?

	H	T	U
	7	5	3
+	2	4	1
	9	9	4

5 535 + 224 = ?

	H	T	U
	5	3	5
+	2	2	4
	7	5	9

6 304 + 264 = ?

	H	T	U
	3	0	4
+	2	6	4
	5	6	8

More practice

Set out these questions yourself to answer them.

7 465 + 123 = ?

H	T	U
4	6	5
+1	2	3
5	8	8

8 842 + 145 = ?

H	T	U
8	4	2
+1	4	5
9	8	7

9 735 + 123 = ?

H	T	U
7	3	5
+1	2	3
8	5	8

10 631 + 264 = ?

H	T	U
6	3	1
+2	6	4
8	9	5

11 455 + 323 = ?

H	T	U
4	5	5
+3	2	3
7	7	8

12 573 + 402 = ?

H	T	U
5	7	3
+4	0	2
9	7	5

Problem solving

13 A farmer had 624 sheep. He bought 315 more of them at market. How many sheep has he now?

```
   6 2 4
 + 3 1 5
   9 3 9
```
939

14 Kim had £468 in a bank account. She paid in an extra £221. How much money is in the bank account now?

```
   4 6 8
 + 2 2 1
   6 8 9
```
£689

15 Two numbers have a difference of 233. If the smaller number is 542, what is the larger number?

```
   2 3 3
 + 5 4 2
   7 7 5
```
775

16 604 adults and 173 children went to a football match. How many people is this in total?

```
   6 0 4
 + 1 7 3
   7 7 7
```
777

How did I find Step 2?   ☐ Easy   ☐ OK   ☐ Difficult

8 Schofield & Sims | Written Calculation: Addition Answers

Step 3: Three-digit addition carrying 1 ten

The digits in the units column of these questions have a total that is greater than 9.

See here that 7 add 5 is greater than 9!

	H	T	U
		5	3	7
+		1	4	5

537 + 145 = ?

What to do

1. Start with adding the units. 7 + 5 = 12. Write the 2 in the units column and carry the ten units over to become 1 ten. Write 1 below the answer line, in the tens column.

2. Now add the digits in the tens column and remember to add the 1 ten you carried. 3 tens + 4 tens plus the 1 ten you carried is 8 tens. Write 8 in the tens column.

3. Then add the hundreds digits. 5 + 1 = 6. Write 6 in the hundreds column to complete the answer.

Now you try

1 534 + 158 = 692

2 726 + 234 = 960

3 555 + 415 = 970

4 714 + 257 = 971

5 633 + 239 = 872

6 429 + 165 = 594

More practice

7 836 + 157 = 993

8 548 + 248 = 796

9 409 + 367 = 776

10 735 + 147 = 882

11 538 + 236 = 774

12 324 + 218 = 542

Set out these questions yourself to answer them.

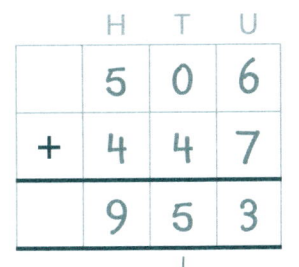

13 435 + 128 = ?

H	T	U
4	3	5
+1	2	8
5	6	3

14 506 + 447 = ?

H	T	U
5	0	6
+4	4	7
9	5	3

15 574 + 406 = ?

H	T	U
5	7	4
+4	0	6
9	8	0

Problem solving

16 Online, a TV costs £548. In a high street shop the same TV costs £128 more. How much does it cost in the shop?

548 + 128 = 676   £676

17 Two numbers have a difference of 733. If the smaller number is 127, what is the larger number?

733 + 127 = 860   860

How did I find Step 3?   ☐ Easy   ☐ OK   ☐ Difficult

10 Schofield & Sims | Written Calculation: Addition Answers

Step 4: Three-digit addition carrying 1 hundred

As for Step 3, these questions have two digits that have a total greater than 9, but this time the digits are in the tens column.
See here that 8 plus 8 is greater than 9!

	H	T	U
	5	8	3
+	2	8	5

What to do

583 + 285 = ?

1. Start at the right-hand side, with the units! Add both units digits. 3 + 5 = 8

	H	T	U
	5	8	3
+	2	8	5
			8

2. Then move left to the tens. 8 + 8 = 16. Write the 6 in the tens column and carry the 10 tens over to become 1 hundred. Write 1 below the line, in the hundreds column.

	H	T	U
	5	8	3
+	2	8	5
		6	8
	1		

3. Now add the digits in the hundreds column and remember to add the 1 you carried. 5 hundreds + 2 hundreds plus the 1 hundred you carried is 8 hundreds. Write 8 in the hundreds column to complete the answer.

	H	T	U
	5	8	3
+	2	8	5
	8	6	8
	1		

Now you try

1
```
    5 8 3
  + 1 4 2
    7 2 5
    1
```

2
```
    6 7 3
  + 2 7 6
    9 4 9
    1
```

3
```
    7 8 2
  + 1 8 5
    9 6 7
    1
```

4
```
    4 5 4
  + 2 8 2
    7 3 6
    1
```

5
```
    3 9 1
  + 3 8 6
    7 7 7
    1
```

6
```
    4 6 2
  + 1 7 7
    6 3 9
    1
```

More practice

7
```
   6 8 5
+  2 4 4
---------
   9 2 9
```

8
```
   3 7 2
+  2 3 4
---------
   6 0 6
```

9
```
   4 6 1
+  4 5 7
---------
   9 1 8
```

Set out these questions yourself to answer them.

10 473 + 174 = ?

H	T	U
4	7	3
+1	7	4
6	4	7

11 382 + 264 = ?

H	T	U
3	8	2
+2	6	4
6	4	6

12 742 + 192 = ?

H	T	U
7	4	2
+1	9	2
9	3	4

Problem solving

13 What is 452 more than 396?

```
   4 5 2
+  3 9 6
---------
   8 4 8
```
848

14 A touch-screen computer costs £352 in a sale. The sale price is £184 less than it was before the sale. How much did it cost before the sale?

```
   3 5 2
+  1 8 4
---------
   5 3 6
```
£536

15 Ahmed climbed a mountain. He stopped for a rest 475m above sea level. The summit of the mountain was 392m higher than he was at that point. How high above sea level was the summit?

```
   4 7 5
+  3 9 2
---------
   8 6 7
```
867m

How did I find Step 4? ☐ Easy   ☐ OK   ☐ Difficult

12 Schofield & Sims | Written Calculation: **Addition** Answers

Step 5: Three-digit addition carrying once, including answers greater than 999

On these pages, you must decide whether to carry a ten and/or a hundred. Look for when the digits in a column have a total greater than 9. Also, answers on these pages may be greater than 999.

What to do

673 + 655 = ?

1. Start at the right-hand side, with the units! Add both units digits.
   3 + 5 = 8

Th	H	T	U
	6	7	3
+	6	5	5
			8

2. Then move left to the tens. 7 + 5 = 12. Write the 2 in the tens column and carry the 10 tens over to become 1 hundred. Write 1 below the line, in the hundreds column.

	6	7	3
+	6	5	5
		2	8
	1		

3. Now add the digits in the hundreds column and remember to add the 1 you carried. 6 hundreds + 6 hundreds plus the 1 hundred you carried is 13 hundreds. If there are no more digits to add, just write 1 in the thousands column and 3 in the hundreds column to complete the answer.

	6	7	3
+	6	5	5
1	3	2	8
	1		

Now you try

1
```
    2 3 6
+   9 4 5
  1 1 8 1
      1
```

2
```
    9 7 4
+   4 6 4
  1 4 3 8
      1
```

3
```
    4 9 3
+   1 9 5
    6 8 8
      1
```

4
```
    6 5 7
+   6 2 4
  1 2 8 1
      1
```

5
```
    7 2 8
+   3 0 6
  1 0 3 4
      1
```

6
```
    8 8 2
+   1 7 4
  1 0 5 6
      1
```

More practice

Set out these questions yourself to answer them.

7 678 + 714 = ?

Th	H	T	U
	6	7	8
+		7	1	4
1	3	9	2

8 384 + 225 = ?

H	T	U
3	8	4
+ 2	2	5
6	0	9

9 918 + 712 = ?

Th	H	T	U
	9	1	8
+	7	1	2
1	6	3	0

Problem solving

10 Work out the missing digit in this addition.

	4	(5)	9
+	9	2	5
1	3	8	4

11 What is the sum of 825 and 567?

```
    8 2 5
+   5 6 7
  1 3 9 2
```
1392

12 A school has 375 girls and 432 boys. How many pupils does it have in total?

```
    3 7 5
+   4 3 2
    8 0 7
```
807

13 How many is 426 plus 849?

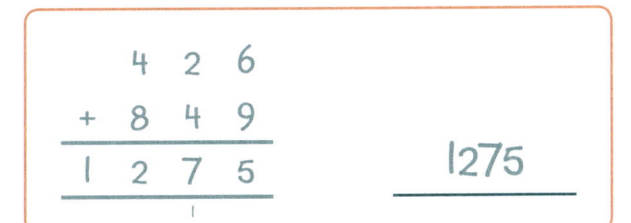

```
    4 2 6
+   8 4 9
  1 2 7 5
```
1275

14 Class M did a traffic survey. They saw 563 cars and 518 other vehicles in one day. How many vehicles did they see altogether that day?

```
    5 6 3
+   5 1 8
  1 0 8 1
```
1081

How did I find Step 5? ☐ Easy ☐ OK ☐ Difficult

Step 6: Three-digit addition of three numbers carrying once

On these pages, the questions involve adding three numbers. This means that sometimes you must carry more than 1 ten or more than 1 hundred.

What to do

$629 + 619 + 233 = ?$

1 Start at the right-hand side, with the units! Add all the units digits. 9 + 9 + 3 = 21. Write the 1 in the units column and carry the 20 over to become 2 tens. Write 2 below the line, in the tens column.

	Th	H	T	U
		6	2	9
		6	1	9
+		2	3	3
				1
			2	

2 Now add the digits in the tens column and remember to add the 2 you carried. 2 tens + 1 ten + 3 tens plus the 2 tens carried = 8 tens. Write the 8 in the tens column.

		6	2	9
		6	1	9
+		2	3	3
			8	1
		2		

3 Now add the hundreds digits. 6 hundreds + 6 hundreds + 2 hundreds = 14 hundreds. If there are no more digits to add, just write 1 in the thousands column and 4 in the hundreds column to complete the answer.

		6	2	9
		6	1	9
+		2	3	3
1	4	8	1	
		2		

Now you try

1
```
    7 4 8
    5 0 8
  + 1 2 8
  1 3 8 4
      2
```

2
```
    5 3 7
    5 3 3
  + 4 2 2
  1 4 9 2
    1
```

3
```
    8 7 2
    2 7 0
  + 1 7 3
  1 3 1 5
      2
```

4
```
    3 9 4
    3 5 1
  + 1 9 3
    9 3 8
      2
```

5
```
    7 1 8
    3 4 8
  + 2 1 4
  1 2 8 0
    2
```

6
```
    9 7 6
    7 4 1
  + 5 4 2
  2 2 5 9
    1
```

Schofield & Sims | Written Calculation: **Addition** Answers   **15**

More practice

Set out these questions yourself to answer them.

7 514 + 207 + 228 = ?

	Th	H	T	U
		5	1	4
		2	0	7
+		2	2	8
		9	4	9
			1	

8 781 + 282 + 196 = ?

	Th	H	T	U
		7	8	1
		2	8	2
+		1	9	6
	1	2	5	9
			2	

Problem solving

9 Can you work out what digits the letters A and B stand for in this addition?

	A	B	A
	B	B	A
+	B	B	A
D	A	C	B
		D	

A = 3 and B = 9

10 164 men, 173 women and 271 children were at a concert. How many people is that altogether?

```
    1 6 4
    1 7 3
 +  2 7 1
    6 0 8
      2
```

608

11 Mrs Brown put 245g of flour, 108g of sugar and 225g of butter into a bowl and mixed it. How heavy is the mixture in total?

```
    2 4 5
    1 0 8
 +  2 2 5
    5 7 8
        1
```

578g

How did I find Step 6? ☐ Easy ☐ OK ☐ Difficult

Schofield & Sims | Written Calculation: Addition Answers

Check-up test 1 — Two- and three-digit addition, including carrying once

Step 1

1 72 + 26 = ?

```
   7 2
+  2 6
   9 8
```

2 55 + 23 = ?

```
   5 5
+  2 3
   7 8
```

3 63 + 24 = ?

```
   6 3
+  2 4
   8 7
```

Step 2

4 543 + 251 = ?

```
   5 4 3
+  2 5 1
   7 9 4
```

5 732 + 234 = ?

```
   7 3 2
+  2 3 4
   9 6 6
```

6 134 + 464 = ?

```
   1 3 4
+  4 6 4
   5 9 8
```

Step 3

7 428 + 358 = ?

```
   4 2 8
+  3 5 8
   7 8 6
     1
```

8 429 + 165 = ?

```
   4 2 9
+  1 6 5
   5 9 4
     1
```

9 635 + 128 = ?

```
   6 3 5
+  1 2 8
   7 6 3
     1
```

Steps 4 and 5

10 391 + 386 = ?

```
   3 9 1
+  3 8 6
   7 7 7
     1
```

11 462 + 977 = ?

```
   4 6 2
+  9 7 7
 1 4 3 9
   1
```

12 775 + 474 = ?

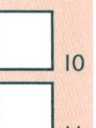

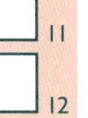

```
   7 7 5
+  4 7 4
 1 2 4 9
   1
```

Step 6

13 718 + 348 + 214 = ?

```
    7 1 8
    3 4 8
  + 2 1 4
  -------
  1 2 8 0
      2
```

14 855 + 741 + 542 = ?

```
    8 5 5
    7 4 1
  + 5 4 2
  -------
  2 1 3 8
    1
```

Steps 1 to 6 mixed

Use the grid below for working.

15 The height of Sue's cat is 25cm. Sue's dog is 61cm taller than her cat. What is the height of her dog?   86cm

16 An iPad costs £352 online. In a shop it costs £184 more than this. What does it cost in the shop?   £536

17 How many more than one thousand is the total of 281, 456 and 302?   39

```
15)    6 1
     + 2 5
       ---
       8 6
```

```
16)    3 5 2
     + 1 8 4
       -----
       5 3 6
         1
```

```
17)    2 8 1
       4 5 6
     + 3 0 2
       -----
     1 0 3 9
         1
```

Total test score

Score	1	2	3	4	5	6	7	8	9	10	11	12	13	14	15	16	17
%	6	12	18	24	29	35	41	47	53	59	65	71	76	82	88	94	100

Step 7: Four-digit addition carrying once

Here you will add four-digit numbers. You will need to carry once in each calculation. Look out for when the digits in a column have a total greater than 9.

	Th	H	T	U
		4	7	2	4
+		1	5	3	5

What to do

4724 + 1535 = ?

1. Add the units digits. 4 + 5 = 9

	Th	H	T	U
	4	7	2	4
+	1	5	3	5
				9

2. Then move left to add the tens digits.
   2 tens + 3 tens = 5 tens

	4	7	2	4
+	1	5	3	5
			5	9

3. Now add the digits in the hundreds column.
   7 hundreds + 5 hundreds is 12 hundreds. Write the 2 in the hundreds column and carry the 10 hundreds over to become 1 thousand. Write 1 below the line, in the thousands column.

	4	7	2	4
+	1	5	3	5
		2	5	9
1				

4. Now add the thousands and remember to add the 1 you carried. 4 thousands + 1 thousand plus the 1 thousand you carried is 6 thousands. Write 6 in the thousands column to complete the answer.

	4	7	2	4
+	1	5	3	5
	6	2	5	9
1				

Now you try

1

	4	4	5	8
+	1	4	8	0
	5	9	3	8
		1		

2

	5	6	2	9
+	1	2	1	6
	6	8	4	5
			1	

3

	3	4	7	0
+	3	3	6	3
	6	8	3	3
	1			

4

	4	8	5	3
+	1	7	3	2
	6	5	8	5
	1			

Schofield & Sims | Written Calculation: Addition Answers 19

More practice

5
```
    5 9 2 4
+   1 7 3 2
─────────────
    7 6 5 6
```

6
```
    6 2 9 3
+   3 6 9 1
─────────────
    9 9 8 4
```

Set out these questions yourself to answer them.

7 2461 + 2263 = ?

Th	H	T	U
2	4	6	1
+2	2	6	3
4	7	2	4

8 3925 + 3574 = ?

Th	H	T	U
3	9	2	5
+3	5	7	4
7	4	9	9

Problem solving

9 A pilot travelled 4323km on Monday. He rested on Tuesday and then flew 4762km on Wednesday. How many kilometres was this in total?

```
    4 3 2 3
+   4 7 6 2
─────────────
    9 0 8 5
```
9085km

10 At a rugby match there were 3444 home fans and 1472 away fans. How many fans were there altogether?

```
    3 4 4 4
+   1 4 7 2
─────────────
    4 9 1 6
```
4916

11 Each letter in this sum stands for a different digit. Using spare paper for working, can you work out what each letter could stand for? **BAKE + CAKE = 9828**

E = 4, K = 1, A = 9 and B and C have a total of 8,

so B and C could be 6 and 2 or 5 and 3.

How did I find Step 7? ☐ Easy   ☐ OK   ☐ Difficult

Step 8: Three-digit addition carrying twice

On these pages, you will learn how to carry a ten and a hundred. Look for when the digits in a column have a total greater than 9.

What to do

687 + 585 = ?

1. Start at the right. Add both units digits. 7 + 5 = 12. Write the 2 in the units column and carry the ten units over to become 1 ten. Write 1 below the line, in the tens column.

	Th	H	T	U
		6	8	7
+		5	8	5
				2
			1	

2. Then move left to add the tens digits and remember to add the 1 you carried. 8 tens + 8 tens plus the 1 ten carried is 17 tens. Write the 7 in the tens column and carry the 10 tens over to become 1 hundred. Write 1 below the line, in the hundreds column.

	6	8	7
+	5	8	5
		7	2
	1	1	

3. Now add the digits in the hundreds column and remember to add the 1 you carried. 6 hundreds + 5 hundreds plus the 1 hundred you carried is 12 hundreds. If there are no more digits to add, just write 2 in the hundreds column and 1 in the thousands column to complete the answer.

	6	8	7
+	5	8	5
1	2	7	2
	1	1	

Now you try

1
```
    2 8 6
+   9 4 5
  1 2 3 1
    1 1
```

2
```
    4 6 5
+   1 8 5
    6 5 0
    1 1
```

3
```
    9 7 9
+   4 6 9
  1 4 4 8
    1 1
```

4
```
    9 5 7
+   4 8 7
  1 4 4 4
    1 1
```

5
```
    6 2 8
+   3 7 6
  1 0 0 4
    1 1
```

6
```
    8 8 9
+   9 7 4
  1 8 6 3
    1 1
```

More practice

Set out these questions yourself to answer them.

7 678 + 734 = ?

Th	H	T	U
	6	7	8
+	7	3	4
1	4	1	2

8 988 + 825 = ?

Th	H	T	U
	9	8	8
+	8	2	5
1	8	1	3

9 968 + 732 = ?

Th	H	T	U
	9	6	8
+	7	3	2
1	7	0	0

Problem solving

10 Work out the missing digit in this addition.

	4	(5)	6
+	9	4	5
1	4	0	1

11 What is the sum of 865 and 567?

	8	6	5
+	5	6	7
1	4	3	2

1432

12 Kim has £479 in her bank account. She puts in £285 more. How much is in the account now?

	4	7	9
+	2	8	5
	7	6	4

£764

13 A safari park had 356 visitors on Saturday and 476 on Sunday. How many visitors came in total that weekend?

	3	5	6
+	4	7	6
	8	3	2

832

How did I find Step 8? ☐ Easy   ☐ OK   ☐ Difficult

Step 9: Four-digit addition carrying once or twice

For the questions in this step, you will add four-digit numbers. Sometimes you will need to carry once and sometimes you will need to carry twice. In this example, both the units and hundreds digits have totals greater than 9.

	Th	H	T	U
		6	7	4	4
+		1	5	3	9

What to do

$6744 + 1539 = ?$

1. Add the units digits. 4 + 9 = 13. Write the 3 in the units column and carry the ten units over to become 1 ten. Write 1 below the line, in the tens column.

2. Then move left to add the tens digits and remember to add the 1 you carried. 4 tens + 3 tens plus the 1 ten carried is 8 tens.

3. Now add the digits in the hundreds column. 7 hundreds + 5 hundreds is 12 hundreds. Write the 2 in the hundreds column and carry the 10 hundreds over to become 1 thousand. Write 1 below the line, in the thousands column.

4. Now add the thousands and remember to add the 1 you carried. 6 thousands + 1 thousand plus the 1 thousand you carried is 8 thousands. Write 8 in the thousands column to complete the answer.

Now you try

1.
    4 6 2 9
  + 1 2 8 3
    5 9 1 2

2.
    3 8 2 7
  + 1 6 1 4
    5 4 4 1

3.
    6 2 7 5
  + 1 3 6 8
    7 6 4 3

4.
    4 8 5 3
  + 1 7 6 2
    6 6 1 5

Schofield & Sims | Written Calculation: Addition Answers   23

More practice

5
```
    5 2 9 4
  + 1 6 9 2
  ---------
    6 9 8 6
      ¹
```

6
```
    4 5 8 3
  + 3 6 9 5
  ---------
    8 2 7 8
      ¹ ¹
```

Set out these questions yourself to answer them.

7 2761 + 2263 = ?

Th	H	T	U
2	7	6	1
+2	2	6	3
5	0	2	4
	¹	¹	

8 3928 + 3567 = ?

Th	H	T	U
3	9	2	8
+3	5	6	7
7	4	9	5
	¹	¹	

Problem solving

9 Paul's income last year was £7378. This year it has increased by £1535. How much is it now?

```
    7 3 7 8
  + 1 5 3 5
  ---------
    8 9 1 3
      ¹ ¹
```
£8913

10 At a football match there were 2764 home fans and 1342 away fans. How many fans were there altogether?

```
    2 7 6 4
  + 1 3 4 2
  ---------
    4 1 0 6
      ¹ ¹
```
4106

11 Sales of the music track 'School's Out' last week were 2815. This week sales rose by 1475. How many were sold this week?

```
    2 8 1 5
  + 1 4 7 5
  ---------
    4 2 9 0
      ¹ ¹
```
4290

How did I find Step 9?   ☐ Easy   ☐ OK   ☐ Difficult

Step 10: Three- and four-digit addition carrying once or twice, answers greater than 9999

These questions involve adding three- and four-digit numbers. Make sure you line up the digits in the correct columns. Sometimes the answers will be greater than 9999.

What to do

$9634 + 871 = ?$

1. Write the digits in the correct columns. Add the units digits.
   $4 + 1 = 5$

	TTh	Th	H	T	U
		9	6	3	4
+			8	7	1
					5

2. Then add the tens. 3 tens + 7 tens = 10 tens. Write 0 in the tens column and carry 10 tens over to become 1 hundred.

		9	6	3	4
+			8	7	1
				0	5

3. Now add the hundreds. 6 hundreds + 8 hundreds plus the 1 hundred carried is 15 hundreds. Write the 5 in the hundreds column and carry the 10 hundreds over to become 1 thousand.

		9	6	3	4
+			8	7	1
			5	0	5

4. Add the thousands to the 1 you carried. 9 thousands plus the 1 thousand carried is 10 thousands. Write 0 in the thousands column and 1 in the ten thousands column to complete the answer.

		9	6	3	4
+			8	7	1
	1	0	5	0	5

Now you try

1

		9	7	8	4
+			7	4	5
	1	0	5	2	9

2

		4	8	2	6
+		6	8	7	1
	1	1	6	9	7

3

		9	5	3	4
+			7	2	8
	1	0	2	6	2

4

		7	9	6	7
+		7	4	7	1
	1	5	4	3	8

More practice

Set out these questions yourself to answer them.

5 9261 + 863 = ?

TTh	Th	H	T	U
	9	2	6	1
+		8	6	3
1	0	1	2	4

6 8925 + 3574 = ?

TTh	Th	H	T	U
	8	9	2	5
+	3	5	7	4
1	2	4	9	9

7 9346 + 2923 = ?

TTh	Th	H	T	U
	9	3	4	6
+	2	9	2	3
1	2	2	6	9

8 9823 + 757 = ?

TTh	Th	H	T	U
	9	8	2	3
+		7	5	7
1	0	5	8	0

Problem solving

9 Phelim wants to buy a car and is looking at two of them. One costs £9574 and the other is £674 more. How much does the more expensive car cost?

```
    9 5 7 4
+     6 7 4
  1 0 2 4 8
```
£10 248

10 8753 people visited the Multiplex cinema during one week in October. 2724 more than this visited in one week in November. How many visited in the November week?

```
    8 7 5 3
+   2 7 2 4
  1 1 4 7 7
```
11 477

How did I find Step 10? ☐ Easy ☐ OK ☐ Difficult

Step 11: Four-digit addition carrying three times

Now you're confident in carrying, you can do it several times. Here, these questions involve carrying three times. Some answers will also be over 9999.

What to do

8634 + 4868 = ?

1. Add the units digits and carry. 4 + 8 = 12

2. Then add the tens. 3 tens + 6 tens plus the 1 ten carried is 10 tens. Write 0 in the tens column and carry 10 tens over to become 1 hundred.

3. Now add the hundreds. 6 hundreds + 8 hundreds plus the 1 hundred carried is 15 hundreds. Write the 5 in the hundreds column and carry the 10 hundreds over to become 1 thousand.

4. Add the thousands. 8 thousands + 4 thousands plus the 1 thousand carried is 13 thousands. Write 3 in the thousands column and 1 in the ten thousands column to complete the answer.

Now you try

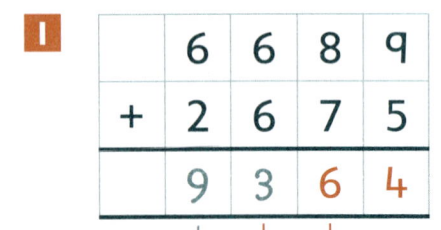

1. 6689 + 2675 = 9364

2. 4826 + 6875 = 11701

3. 6538 + 4798 = 11336

4. 9887 + 7576 = 17463

Schofield & Sims | Written Calculation: Addition Answers — 27

More practice

Set out these questions yourself to answer them.

5 9698 + 7863 = ?

TTh	Th	H	T	U
	9	6	9	8
+	7	8	6	3
1	7	5	6	1

6 7975 + 3576 = ?

TTh	Th	H	T	U
	7	9	7	5
+	3	5	7	6
1	1	5	5	1

Problem solving

7 A, B and C have been used to replace three digits in this addition. Can you work out the value of A, B and C?

A = 9   B = 8   C = 7

	A	C	B	A
+	A	C	B	A
1	9	5	C	B

8 A pilot flew 3752 miles in January and 4589 miles in February. How many miles did he fly altogether?

```
   3 7 5 2
 + 4 5 8 9
   8 3 4 1
```
8341 miles

9 What is the total of 5769 and 6856?

```
   5 7 6 9
 + 6 8 5 6
 1 2 6 2 5
```
12 625

10 Last year Sarah cycled 4337km. This year she cycled 1965km more than last year. How many kilometres did she cycle this year?

```
   4 3 3 7
 + 1 9 6 5
   6 3 0 2
```
6302km

How did I find Step 11?   ☐ Easy   ☐ OK   ☐ Difficult

Step 12: Addition of three numbers with three and four digits carrying up to three times

In this step, you'll add several numbers. Make sure you write the digits into the correct columns first. Remember to carry digits when necessary.

What to do

8794 + 868 + 7642 = ?

1. Add the units digits and carry. 4 + 8 + 2 = 14

TTh	Th	H	T	U
	8	7	9	4
		8	6	8
+	7	6	4	2
				4
			1	

2. Then add the tens. 9 tens + 6 tens + 4 tens plus the 1 ten carried is 20 tens. Write 0 in the tens column and carry 20 tens over to become 2 hundreds.

TTh	Th	H	T	U
	8	7	9	4
		8	6	8
+	7	6	4	2
			0	4
		2	1	

3. Now add the hundreds. 7 hundreds + 8 hundreds + 6 hundreds plus the 2 hundreds carried is 23 hundreds. Write the 3 in the hundreds column and carry the 20 hundreds over to become 2 thousands.

TTh	Th	H	T	U
	8	7	9	4
		8	6	8
+	7	6	4	2
		3	0	4
	2	2	1	

4. Add the thousands to the 2 thousands you carried. 8 thousands + 7 thousands plus the 2 thousands carried is 17 thousands. Write 7 in the thousands column and 1 in the ten thousands column to complete the answer.

TTh	Th	H	T	U
	8	7	9	4
		8	6	8
+	7	6	4	2
1	7	3	0	4
	2	2	1	

Now you try

Set out these questions yourself to answer them.

1 5886 + 697 + 975 = ?

TTh	Th	H	T	U
	5	8	8	6
		6	9	7
+		9	7	5
	7	5	5	8
	2	2	1	

2 7864 + 2856 + 774 = ?

TTh	Th	H	T	U
	7	8	6	4
	2	8	5	6
+		7	7	4
1	1	4	9	4
	2	1	1	

More practice Use the grid below for working.

3 2674 + 663 + 1845 = ? _5182_

4 7841 + 4278 + 953 = ? _13 072_

5 7459 + 708 + 478 = ? _8645_

6 9573 + 3867 + 858 = ? _14 298_

```
3)    2 6 7 4         4)      7 8 4 1
        6 6 3                  4 2 7 8
    + 1 8 4 5              +     9 5 3
      5 1 8 2              1 3 0 7 2
        2 1 1                  2 1 1

5)    7 4 5 9         6)      9 5 7 3
        7 0 8                  3 8 6 7
    +   4 7 8              +     8 5 8
      8 6 4 5              1 4 2 9 8
        1 1 2                  2 1 1
```

Problem solving

7 Choose a single digit greater than 3. Repeat it to make two four-digit numbers and a three-digit number. Then find the sum of the numbers, for example 4444 + 4444 + 444. Do this for 5, 6, 7, 8 and 9 too. What do you notice about the digits of the answers? Use spare paper for working.

_9332, 11 665, 13 998, 16 331, 18 664, 20 997_

The tens and hundreds digits are the same.

How did I find Step 12? ☐ Easy   ☐ OK   ☐ Difficult

Check-up test 2 — Three- and four-digit addition, with up to three carries

Step 7

1 4855 + 1814 = ?

```
   4 8 5 5
+  1 8 1 4
---------
   6 6 6 9
```

2 4335 + 2381 = ?

```
   4 3 3 5
+  2 3 8 1
---------
   6 7 1 6
```

Step 8

3 627 + 377 = ?

```
   6 2 7
+  3 7 7
-------
 1 0 0 4
```

4 495 + 848 = ?

```
   4 9 5
+  8 4 8
-------
 1 3 4 3
```

Step 9

5 5948 + 1731 = ?

```
   5 9 4 8
+  1 7 3 1
---------
   7 6 7 9
```

6 5761 + 2263 = ?

```
   5 7 6 1
+  2 2 6 3
---------
   8 0 2 4
```

Steps 10 and 11

7 4439 + 497 = ?

```
   4 4 3 9
+    4 9 7
---------
   4 9 3 6
```

8 5452 + 2768 = ?

```
   5 4 5 2
+  2 7 6 8
---------
   8 2 2 0
```

Step 12

Use the grid below for working.

9 2374 + 2265 + 845 = ?   5484

10 7664 + 725 + 1953 = ?   10 342

```
9)     2 3 7 4          10)    7 6 6 4
       2 2 6 5                   7 2 5
   +     8 4 5              + 1 9 5 3
       ─────────              ─────────
       5 4 8 4              1 0 3 4 2
         1 1 1                2   1 1
```

Steps 7 to 12 mixed

Use the grid below for working.

11 What is the total of 5769 and 6856?   12 625

12 The price of a TV that cost £757 was increased by £176. What is the new price?   £933

13 Add 668 to 1757.   2425

14 Which year was 945 years after the year 1066?   2011

```
11)    5 7 6 9          12)      7 5 7
   + 6 8 5 6                +    1 7 6
     ─────────                   ─────────
   1 2 6 2 5                     9 3 3
       1 1 1                       1 1

13)      6 6 8          14)    1 0 6 6
   + 1 7 5 7                +    9 4 5
     ─────────                  ─────────
     2 4 2 5                    2 0 1 1
       1 1 1                        1 1
```

Total test score

Score	1	2	3	4	5	6	7	8	9	10	11	12	13	14
%	7	14	21	29	36	43	50	57	64	71	79	86	93	100

14

Step 13: Five-digit addition carrying up to four times

What to do

1. Now that you're used to carrying, you can add larger and larger numbers. These questions involve adding five-digit numbers.

2. Just remember to work from right to left and carry digits when necessary.

	HTh	TTh	Th	H	T	U
		5	9	6	3	4
+		6	7	8	7	1
	1	2	7	5	0	5

Now you try

1
```
    3 7 6 3 4
+   6 7 2 4 9
  1 0 4 8 8 3
```

2
```
    4 5 7 3 8
+   7 3 5 7 3
  1 1 9 3 1 1
```

3
```
    6 6 3 8 4
+   3 5 8 7 2
  1 0 2 2 5 6
```

4
```
    5 9 6 3 6
+   4 5 4 7 4
  1 0 5 1 1 0
```

5
```
    9 9 2 2 7
+   7 3 6 8 4
  1 7 2 9 1 1
```

6
```
    8 5 4 9 9
+   8 7 4 2 0
  1 7 2 9 1 9
```

Schofield & Sims | Written Calculation: Addition Answers 33

More practice

7
```
   8 4 5 0 6
+  1 4 8 9 6
───────────
   9 9 4 0 2
```

8
```
   7 7 7 7 7
+  7 7 7 7 7
───────────
 1 5 5 5 5 4
```

Set out these questions yourself to answer them.

9 79 837 + 57 842 = ?

HTh	TTh	Th	H	T	U
	7	9	8	3	7
+ 5	7	8	4	2
1	3	7	6	7	9

10 59 094 + 71 887 = ?

HTh	TTh	Th	H	T	U
	5	9	0	9	4
+ 7	1	8	8	7
1	3	0	9	8	1

Problem solving

11 Palindromic numbers are those that are the same when the digits are written in reverse order, like 15551 or 23532. Use two digits to make two palindromic numbers, for example 37773 and 73337. Add them to find the total. Is the answer palindromic? Try other digits in the same way. Can you find any palindromic answers?
Use spare paper for working.

> Only if the two digits have a total of 11 or a total less than 10,
> for example 5 and 6 or 1 and 7.

12 25 753 fans were at a football stadium to see a match and 94 545 fans watched it on TV. How many saw the match in total?

```
   2 5 7 5 3
+  9 4 5 4 5
───────────
 1 2 0 2 9 8
```
120 298

How did I find Step 13?   ☐ Easy   ☐ OK   ☐ Difficult

Step 14: Addition of a list of numbers

It is important to be able to add a long list of numbers. Make sure when you set out the addition that you write the digits into the correct columns first.

What to do

1. Line up the digits correctly.

2. Then work from right to left, adding the digits in each column and carrying if necessary. Look for pairs or sets of numbers that total 10 to help you add them.

3. Remember to add the carried digit when adding the digits in the next column.

Find the sum of 47 353, 573, 6856, 252 and 12 453.

	HTh	TTh	Th	H	T	U
			4	7	3	5	3
				5	7	3
				6	8	5	6
					2	5	2
+		1	2	4	5	3
		6	7	4	8	7
		1	2	2	1

Now you try Set out these questions yourself to answer them.

1 Find the total of 54 845, 8346, 9487, 171 and 14 653.

HTh	TTh	Th	H	T	U
	5	4	8	4	5
		8	3	4	6
		9	4	8	7
			1	7	1
+	1	4	6	5	3
	8	7	5	0	2
	2	2	3	2

2 Find the sum of 8243, 25 573, 1256, 609 and 81 253.

HTh	TTh	Th	H	T	U
			8	2	4	3
	2	5	5	7	3
		1	2	5	6
			6	0	9
+	8	1	2	5	3
1	1	6	9	3	4
1	1	2	2

More practice Use the grid below for working.

3 21 574 + 663 + 1 845 + 53 524 + 3 442 = ?   81 048

4 5 459 + 17 308 + 478 + 6 846 + 88 445 = ?   118 536

```
3)    2 1 5 7 4          4)       5 4 5 9
        6 6 3                   1 7 3 0 8
      1 8 4 5                       4 7 8
    5 3 5 2 4                     6 8 4 6
  +   3 4 4 2                 + 8 8 4 4 5
    8 1 0 4 8                   1 1 8 5 3 6
      1 3 2 1                       2 2 2 3
```

Problem solving

5 Use spare paper to find the sum of 11 111, 22 222, 33 333, 44 444 and 55 555.
Write the answer in digits and in words.

166 665

one hundred and sixty-six thousand, six hundred and sixty-five

6 This table shows the number of copies of a newspaper that was sold each day. Find the total number sold in the week.

Mon	Tues	Wed	Thurs	Fri	Sat	Sun
6846	4675	8465	4662	5102	18352	25432

```
    6 8 4 6
    4 6 7 5
    8 4 6 5
    4 6 6 2
    5 1 0 2
  1 8 3 5 2
+ 2 5 4 3 2
  7 3 5 3 4
    4 3 3 2
```
73 534

How did I find Step 14? ☐ Easy ☐ OK ☐ Difficult

Step 15: Large number addition

What to do

1. You've learnt how to do written addition for numbers with up to five digits. Adding even larger numbers is just as easy!
2. Remember to work from right to left and carry digits when necessary.

```
       HTh TTh  Th   H   T   U
              5   0   6   6   4   1
          +   2   4   8   2   7   3
              7   5   4   9   1   4
                      1       1
```

Now you try

1 Seven hundred and nine thousand, three hundred and seventeen plus thirty-one thousand, four hundred and forty-six.

```
   HTh TTh  Th   H   T   U
     7   0   9   3   1   7
 +       3   1   4   4   6
     7   4   0   7   6   3
             1       1
```

2 Nine hundred and twenty thousand, three hundred and fifty add six hundred and eighty-two thousand and eighteen.

```
 M  HTh TTh  Th   H   T   U
         9   2   0   3   5   0
     +   6   8   2   0   1   8
     1   6   0   2   3   6   8
             1
```

3 Eight hundred thousand, five hundred and twelve plus two hundred and sixty thousand, two hundred and nineteen.

```
 M  HTh TTh  Th   H   T   U
         8   0   0   5   1   2
     +   2   6   0   2   1   9
     1   0   6   0   7   3   1
                         1
```

4 Two hundred and sixty-one thousand, nine hundred and three add ninety-four thousand, six hundred and seven.

```
   HTh TTh  Th   H   T   U
     2   6   1   9   0   3
 +           9   4   6   0   7
     3   5   6   5   1   0
         1       1       1
```

More practice

Set out these questions yourself to answer them.

5 Six hundred and ninety thousand and thirty-nine plus seventy-eight thousand, two hundred and forty-one.

	HTh	TTh	Th	H	T	U
	6	9	0	0	3	9
+		7	8	2	4	1
	7	6	8	2	8	0

6 Five hundred and twelve thousand and forty-six add six hundred and nine thousand and sixty-five.

M	HTh	TTh	Th	H	T	U
	5	1	2	0	4	6
+	6	0	9	0	6	5
1	1	2	1	1	1	1

Problem solving

7 Can you work out which digit the letter A stands for in this addition?

A = 4

	9	A	8	A	7	5
+	6	8	2	8	A	6
1	6	3	1	3	2	1

8 Two large schools raised money for a children's charity. One school raised £385 057 and the other raised £184 488. How much did they give to the charity altogether?

```
    3 8 5 0 5 7
+   1 8 4 4 8 8
    5 6 9 5 4 5
```
£569 545

9 Over a season, 573 684 adults and 375 427 children went to watch the matches of a football team. What was the total attendance?

```
    5 7 3 6 8 4
+   3 7 5 4 2 7
    9 4 9 1 1 1
```
949 111

How did I find Step 15? ☐ Easy ☐ OK ☐ Difficult

38 Schofield & Sims | Written Calculation: **Addition** Answers

Check-up test 3 Addition of large numbers

Step 13

1 44638 + 74677 = ?

```
   4 4 6 3 8
+  7 4 6 7 7
-----------
 1 1 9 3 1 5
     1 1 1
```

2 69094 + 71887 = ?

```
   6 9 0 9 4
+  7 1 8 8 7
-----------
 1 4 0 9 8 1
     1 1 1
```

Step 14

3 Find the sum of 67354, 573, 6856, 252 and 12453.

```
   6 7 3 5 4
       5 7 3
     6 8 5 6
       2 5 2
+  1 2 4 5 3
-----------
   8 7 4 8 8
     1 2 2 1
```

4 Find the sum of 9354, 25473, 1256, 509 and 81253.

```
     9 3 5 4
   2 5 4 7 3
     1 2 5 6
       5 0 9
+  8 1 2 5 3
-----------
 1 1 7 8 4 5
   1 1 2 2
```

Step 15

5 Nine hundred and twenty-seven thousand, three hundred and fifty plus six hundred and eighty-two thousand, eight hundred and eighteen.

```
   9 2 7 3 5 0
+  6 8 2 8 1 8
-------------
 1 6 1 0 1 6 8
     1 1 1
```

6 Five hundred and twelve thousand and thirty-nine plus seven hundred and nine thousand and sixty-five.

```
   5 1 2 0 3 9
+  7 0 9 0 6 5
-------------
 1 2 2 1 1 0 4
     1   1 1
```

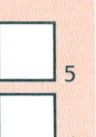

Schofield & Sims | Written Calculation: **Addition** Answers **39**

Steps 13 to 15 mixed

Use the grid below for working.

7 54 753 fans were at a football stadium to see a match and 58 545 fans watched it on TV. How many saw the match in total? _113 298_

8 Over a season 439 684 adults and 327 427 children went to watch the matches of a hockey team. What was the total attendance? _767 111_

9 This table shows the number of children attending a school each day. Find the total attendance for the week. _11 696_

Mon	2342
Tues	2355
Wed	2314
Thurs	2347
Fri	2338

```
7)    5 4 7 5 3        8)    4 3 9 6 8 4
   +  5 8 5 4 5           +  3 2 7 4 2 7
      1 1 3 2 9 8            7 6 7 1 1 1
          1 1                    1 1 1 1

9)    2 3 4 2
      2 3 5 5
      2 3 1 4
      2 3 4 7
   +  2 3 3 8
      1 1 6 9 6
          1 1 2
```

Total test score

Score	1	2	3	4	5	6	7	8	9
%	11	22	33	44	56	67	78	89	100

Step 16: Decimal addition one decimal place

Now that you can add whole numbers, adding decimals is almost as easy! All you need to do is to set out the digits in the correct columns and add in the same way!

	Th	H	T	U . t
		3	4	4 . 5
+			1	8 . 4

What to do

344.5 + 18.4 = ?

1. Start with the right-hand column, the tenths.
   5 tenths + 4 tenths = 9 tenths

	Th	H	T	U . t
		3	4	4 . 5
+			1	8 . 4
				. 9

2. Then move to the units. 4 + 8 = 12. Write 2 and carry the 10.

		3	4	4 . 5
+			1	8 . 4
				2 . 9
			1	

3. Continue working left to complete the addition. Remember to put the decimal point in your answer, in line with the decimal points above.

		3	4	4 . 5
+			1	8 . 4
		3	6	2 . 9
			1	

Now you try

1 5197.4 + 432.7 = ?

	5	1	9	7 . 4
+		4	3	2 . 7
	5	6	3	0 . 1

2 455.9 + 78.4 = ?

		4	5	5 . 9
+			7	8 . 4
		5	3	4 . 3

3 3527.4 + 1278.3 = ?

	3	5	2	7 . 4
+	1	2	7	8 . 3
	4	8	0	5 . 7

4 704.3 + 437.9 = ?

		7	0	4 . 3
+		4	3	7 . 9
	1	1	4	2 . 2

More practice

Set out these questions yourself to answer them.

5 8526.4 + 495.8 = ?

	Th	H	T	U . t
	8	5	2	6 . 4
+		4	9	5 . 8
	9	0	2	2 . 2

6 8763.1 + 532.7 = ?

	Th	H	T	U . t
	8	7	6	3 . 1
+		5	3	2 . 7
	9	2	9	5 . 8

Problem solving

7 Melina runs 67.6km in January and 7.7km further than this in February. How far does she run in February?

```
   6 7.6
+    7.7
   7 5.3
```
75.3km

8 In an 800m athletics race, the time of the fastest runner was 156.6 seconds. The slowest runner took 18.9 seconds longer. How long did the slowest runner take?

```
  1 5 6.6
+   1 8.9
  1 7 5.5
```
175.5 seconds

9 After going on a diet, Sam weighed 78.8kg. Before the diet his weight had been 13.5kg more than this. How much did he weigh before the diet?

```
   7 8.8
+  1 3.5
   9 2.3
```
92.3kg

How did I find Step 16? ☐ Easy ☐ OK ☐ Difficult

Step 17: Decimal addition two decimal places

Here you will add numbers with two decimal places.
Remember to set out the digits in the correct columns.

	H	T	U .	t	h
	1	6	2 .	3	8
+		1	8 .	6	7

$162.38 + 18.67 = ?$

What to do

1. Start with the right-hand column. 8 hundredths + 7 hundredths is 15 hundredths. Write the 5 hundredths and carry the 10 hundredths as 1 tenth.

	H	T	U .	t	h
	1	6	2 .	3	8
+		1	8 .	6	7
					5

2. 3 tenths + 6 tenths plus the 1 tenth carried is 10 tenths. Write the 0. Carry the 10 tenths as 1 unit.

		1	6	2 .	3	8
+			1	8 .	6	7
					0	5

3. Then move to the units. 2 + 8 plus the 1 carried is 11. Write 1 and carry the ten.

		1	6	2 .	3	8
+			1	8 .	6	7
				1	0	5

4. Continue working left to complete the addition. Remember to put the decimal point in your answer, in line with the decimal points above.

		1	6	2 .	3	8
+			1	8 .	6	7
		1	8	1 .	0	5

Now you try

1 $513.64 + 131.77 = ?$

	5	1	3 .	6	4
+	1	3	1 .	7	7
	6	4	5 .	4	1

2 $235.94 + 67.84 = ?$

	2	3	5 .	9	4
+		6	7 .	8	4
	3	0	3 .	7	8

More practice

3
```
    7 4 5.6 4
+   1 2 8.6 5
  ─────────
    8 7 4.2 9
```

4
```
    8 8 8.8 8
+       2 3.4 3
  ─────────
    9 1 2.3 1
```

Set out these questions yourself to answer them.

5 652.74 + 195.84 = ?

H	T	U . t	h
6	5	2 . 7	4
+1	9	5 . 8	4
8	4	8 . 5	8

6 832.19 + 53.87 = ?

H	T	U . t	h
8	3	2 . 1	9
+	5	3 . 8	7
8	8	6 . 0	6

Problem solving

7 Jack has £546.45 in his bank account. His wages of £375.33 are also paid into this account. How much money does he have now?

```
    5 4 6.4 5
+   3 7 5.3 3
  ─────────
    9 2 1.7 8
```

£921.78

8 What is 37.68ml more than 125.55ml?

```
      3 7.6 8
+   1 2 5.5 5
  ─────────
    1 6 3.2 3
```

163.23ml

9 A baby weighed 3.46kg at birth. At six months old he had gained 4.88kg. How much did he weigh when he was six months old?

```
      3.4 6
+     4.8 8
    ─────
      8.3 4
```

8.34kg

How did I find Step 17? ☐ Easy ☐ OK ☐ Difficult

Step 18: Decimal addition different numbers of decimal places

What to do

In this last step, the questions have different numbers of decimal places so you must be careful to write the digits in the correct columns. Sometimes it can help to write zeros in the empty spaces. Don't forget to put the decimal point in your answer each time!

Now you try Set out these questions yourself to answer them.

1 492.76 + 16.825 = ?

	H	T	U . t	h	th
	4	9	2 . 7	6	0
+		1	6 . 8	2	5
	5	0	9 . 5	8	5

2 205.7 + 52.139 = ?

	H	T	U . t	h	th
	2	0	5 . 7	0	0
+		5	2 . 1	3	9
	2	5	7 . 8	3	9

3 842.9 + 9.82 = ?

	H	T	U . t	h
	8	4	2 . 9	0
+			9 . 8	2
	8	5	2 . 7	2

4 78.135 + 38.66 = ?

	T	U . t	h	th
		7 8 . 1	3	5
+		3 8 . 6	6	0
	1	1 6 . 7	9	5

5 908.8 + 174.631 = ?

	H	T	U . t	h	th
		9	0 8 . 8	0	0
+		1	7 4 . 6	3	1
	1	0	8 3 . 4	3	1

6 809.3 + 562.89 = ?

	H	T	U . t	h
		8	0 9 . 3	0
+		5	6 2 . 8	9
	1	3	7 2 . 1	9

More practice

Set out these questions yourself to answer them. Check your answers by subtracting.

7 4653.75 + 2854.56 = ?

```
   Th  H  T  U . t  h
        4  6  5  3 . 7  5
     +  2  8  5  4 . 5  6
        7  5  0  8 . 3  1
```

8 406.90 + 384.73 = ?

```
        H  T  U . t  h
           4  0  6 . 9  0
        +  3  8  4 . 7  3
           7  9  1 . 6  3
```

Problem solving

9 Kay went on holiday. During the first week she spent £183.87 and in the second week she spent £275.90. How much more than £450 did she spend in total?

```
     1  8  3 . 8  7
  +  2  7  5 . 9  0
     4  5  9 . 7  7
```

£9.77

10 Usain Bolt ran 100m in 9.572 seconds. This was 1.228 seconds faster than the world record holder in 1891. How many seconds did the world record holder in 1891 take?

```
     9 . 5  7  2
  +  1 . 2  2  8
    10 . 8  0  0
```

10.8 seconds

11 What is special about the sum of 304.28 litres and 251.275 litres?

```
     3  0  4 . 2  8  0
  +  2  5  1 . 2  7  5
     5  5  5 . 5  5  5
```

It is 555.555 litres.

The digits are all the same.

How did I find Step 18? ☐ Easy ☐ OK ☐ Difficult

46 Schofield & Sims | Written Calculation: Addition Answers

Final test Addition of whole numbers and decimals

Steps 16 to 18

1 7526.5 + 495.7 = ?

	7	5	2	6 .	5
+		4	9	5 .	7
	8	0	2	2 .	2

2 3727.4 + 1278.9 = ?

	3	7	2	7 .	4
+	1	2	7	8 .	9
	5	0	0	6 .	3

3 567.27 + 164.58 = ?

	5	6	7 .	2	7
+	1	6	4 .	5	8
	7	3	1 .	8	5

4 828.36 + 55.29 = ?

	8	2	8 .	3	6
+		5	5 .	2	9
	8	8	3 .	6	5

5 742.9 + 16.826 = ?

	7	4	2 .	9	0	0
+		1	6 .	8	2	6
	7	5	9 .	7	2	6

6 55.134 + 28.77 = ?

	5	5 .	1	3	4
+	2	8 .	7	7	
	8	3 .	9	0	4

Use the grid below for working.

7 A parcel weighs 2.78kg. Another parcel weighs 1.34kg more. How much does it weigh?   _4.12kg_

8 Add 90.92 to 902.9.   _993.82_

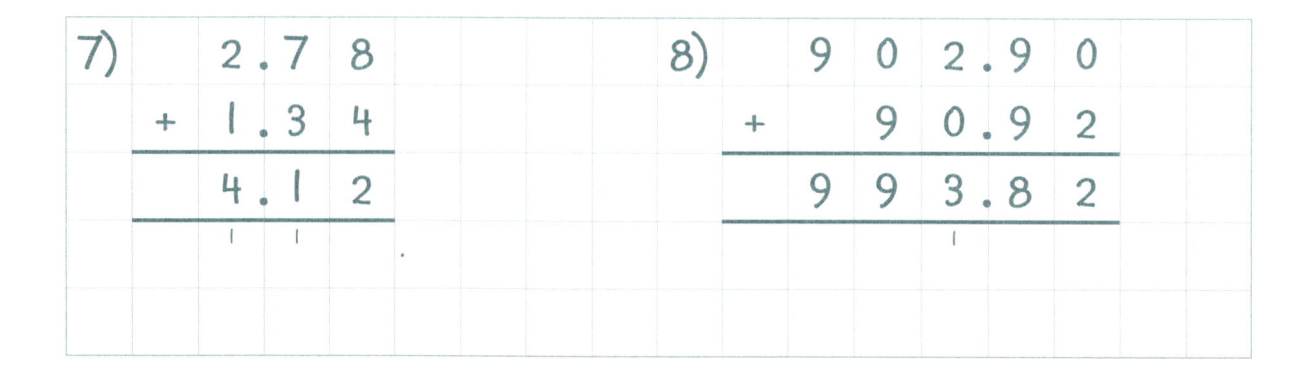

7)		2 .	7	8
	+	1 .	3	4
		4 .	1	2

8)		9	0	2 .	9	0
	+		9	0 .	9	2
		9	9	3 .	8	2

Steps 1 to 18 mixed

Use the grid below for working.

9 How many more than one thousand is the total of 381, 457 and 261?   99

10 Find the sum of 8338 and 3883.   12 221

11 Which year was 935 years after the year 1066?   2001

12 The price of a bike that cost £1257 was increased by £186. What is the new price?   £1443

13 A forestry service planted 50 687 trees last year and 36 779 trees this year. How many trees were planted altogether?   87 466

14 How much did Nigel pay in total for items costing £14.57, £82.34 and £45.17?   £142.08

9)
```
    3 8 1
    4 5 7
  + 2 6 1
  1 0 9 9
```

10)
```
    8 3 3 8
  + 3 8 8 3
  1 2 2 2 1
```

11)
```
      9 3 5
  + 1 0 6 6
    2 0 0 1
```

12)
```
    1 2 5 7
        1 8 6
  + 
    1 4 4 3
```

13)
```
    5 0 6 8 7
  + 3 6 7 7 9
    8 7 4 6 6
```

14)
```
    1 4 . 5 7
    8 2 . 3 4
  + 4 5 . 1 7
  1 4 2 . 0 8
```

Total test score

Score	1	2	3	4	5	6	7	8	9	10	11	12	13	14
%	7	14	21	29	36	43	50	57	64	71	79	86	93	100

Written Calculation — Group record sheet

Pupil Book: _____

Class/Set: _____

Pupil's name	Check-up test 1	Check-up test 2	Check-up test 3	Final test	Assessment test 1*	Assessment test 2*	Mixed calculations test*

*Available as assessment resources in the back of the **Written Calculation: Teacher's Guide** (ISBN 978 07217 1278 9)

From: **Written Calculation: Addition Answers** by Hilary Koll and Steve Mills (ISBN 978 07217 1272 7). Copyright © Schofield & Sims Ltd, 2015. Published by Schofield & Sims Ltd, Dogley Mill, Fenay Bridge, Huddersfield HD8 0NQ, UK (www.schofieldandsims.co.uk). This page may be photocopied after purchase for use within your school or institution only.